T0142668

Don't Be A PUSSY

A politically incorrect book for entitled teens and their traumatized parents.

Written by Elizabeth Jordan

Illustrated by Ash Antchoutine

Copyright © 2022 Elizabeth Jordan.

All rights reserved. No part of this book may be used or reproduced by any means, graphic, electronic, or mechanical, including photocopying, recording, taping or by any information storage retrieval system without the written permission of the author except in the case of brief quotations embodied in critical articles and reviews.

Archway Publishing books may be ordered through booksellers or by contacting:

Archway Publishing
1663 Liberty Drive
Bloomington, IN 47403
www.archwaypublishing.com
844-669-3957

Because of the dynamic nature of the Internet, any web addresses or links contained in this book may have changed since publication and may no longer be valid. The views expressed in this work are solely those of the author and do not necessarily reflect the views of the publisher, and the publisher hereby disclaims any responsibility for them.

ISBN: 978-1-6657-1929-2 (sc)
ISBN: 978-1-6657-1930-8 (hc)
ISBN: 978-1-6657-1931-5 (e)

Print information available on the last page.

Archway Publishing rev. date: 03/04/2022

Don't Be A Pusi

An inappropriate and politically incorrect book
for entitled children and their traumatized parents.

pu·sil·lan·i·mous
/ˌpyo͞osəˈlanəməs/

Learn to pronounce

adjective

showing a lack of courage or determination.

Don't be a Pusi....

And when I say that,
I don't mean a cat,
But more like a grossly over-fed rat.

I mean be a woman or a man, not a louse.
Act politely with pleasure, or get out of my house.

For the last few decades, I've noticed a trend
where we parents are desperate to be our kids' friend.

Now a friend is good, important, and true
But can become an ingredient for a mean witches' brew.

What you kids need to model, to follow, to mimic,
Is a strong parent, not some new gimmick.
Not a new age theory letting kids have their way,
Hoping they'll get by late at night, while you sit home and pray.

A Mom who's a boss, a Dad who's a dude,
Who doesn't allow you to be fucking rude.

Don't ask what your parents can do for you,
But rather say" hey Mom, Dad - what can *I do*?"

As babies you started so sweet so serene..
Our parents warned "Just Wait!
we questioned, "what do you mean?"

We started to tolerate small baby fits
Suddenly staring at teens with braces and zits

We kept you around despite all common sense
We didn't plan ahead to our defense!

It's not meant to be bad.
Just dont make us mad.

Learn how to behave
before you can shave.

For habits are formed at an early age
Be good little kids or sit in a cage.

Remember the old days when parent trumped child
Stay in control, don't act spoiled and wild.

Cut us some slack, we have your back.
Stop acting so cool and talking smack.

One day You'll be raising *your* children too
and thinking "What on earth should I do?"

Why am I sober?
I'd rather be plowed.
Is drinking at noon really not allowed?

Thats no fun for you and no fun for me
Don't force us to play some damn referee.

Just dont be a Pusi, work hard and be kind
Or when we get old we might loose our mind

Then the tables will turn as we age and throw fits
And you'll be stuck cleaning our poopy bits.

Good luck to you all both parent and kid
Try enforcing strict values
As wise grandparents once did.